In praise and celebr...

FRIENDS

A HELEN EXLEY GIFTBOOK

EXLEY

NEW YORK • WATFORD, UK

Best friend,
my well-spring in the wilderness!

GEORGE ELIOT (MARY ANN EVANS)
(1819-1880)

Two people, yes, two lasting friends,
The giving comes, the taking ends.
There is no measure for such things,
For this all Nature slows and sings.

ELIZABETH JENNINGS,
FROM "FRIENDSHIP"

Friendship! Mysterious cement of the soul!
Sweetener of life!

ROBERT BLAIR
(1699-1747)

Friendship is a sheltering tree.

SAMUEL TAYLOR COLERIDGE
(1772-1834)

Happiness is my friend's hand.

GILLIAN QUEEN, AGE 10

my friend

A fire gives warmth and light,
and likewise a friend.
When I see him
I feel the joy deep inside me,
like a pilgrim
who is lost and finds
the right way at last.

G. LAENEN

[Friends] cherish each other's hopes.

They are kind to each other's dreams.

HENRY DAVID THOREAU
(1817-1862)

Friends, companions, lovers,

are those who treat us

in terms of our unlimited worth

to ourselves.

HENRY ALONZO MYERS

One DOES NOT MAKE FRIENDS;
ONE RECOGNIZES THEM.

ISABEL PATERSON

Friendship is based on

chemistry and trust. . .

and why it happens

or why it rises and falls,

and rises again,

is a mystery,

like a fine piece of music.

RICHARD LOUV,
FROM "THE WEB OF LIFE"

I love you not only for what you are,
but for what I am when I am with you.

I love you not only for what you have made of yourself,
but for what you are making of me.

I love you because you have done more than
any creed could have done to make me good,
and more than any fate could have done to
make me happy.

You have done it without a touch,
without a word, without a sign.

You have done it by being yourself.
Perhaps that is what being a friend means, after all.

ROY CROFT

The glory of friendship is not the
outstretched hand, nor
the kindly smile nor the joy of companionship;
it is the spirited inspiration that comes
to one when he discovers that someone else
believes in him and is willing to trust him
with his friendship.

RALPH WALDO EMERSON
(1 8 0 3 - 1 8 8 2)

Two friends playing together.

And love is when you like to play when he wants to

and you may not want to.

DAVID WILSON, AGE 7

It is not that a person has occasion often
to fall back upon the kindness of friends;
perhaps we may never experience the necessity of doing so;
but we are governed by our imaginations,
and they stand there as a solid
and impregnable bulwark against all the evils of life.

SYDNEY SMITH
(1771-1845)

IT DIDN'T MATTER
THAT SOME OF THOSE FRIENDS
WHO WERE THERE FOR US WERE FRIENDS
WE HAD NOT SEEN OFTEN.
WHAT MATTERED
IS THAT WHEN WE NEEDED THEM,
THE TIE WAS THERE.
AND THEY CAME TO HELP
IN ANY WAY THEY COULD.

NINA TOTENBERG

Then little by little we discover one friend,
in the midst of the crowd of friends,
who is particularly happy to be with us
and to whom, we realize,
we have an infinite number of things to say:
She is not the top of the class,
she is not particularly well thought of
by the others, she does not wear showy clothes...
and when we are walking home with her
we realize that her shoes are identical to ours –
strong and simple, not showy and flimsy
like those of our other friends....

NATALIA GINZBURG, b.1916,
FROM "THE LITTLE VIRTUES"

One friend will do.

PAM BROWN, b.1928

FRIENDSHIP IS BY ITS VERY NATURE
FREER OF DECEIT THAN ANY OTHER RELATIONSHIP
WE CAN KNOW BECAUSE IT IS THE BOND LEAST AFFECTED
BY STRIVING FOR POWER, PHYSICAL PLEASURE,
OR MATERIAL PROFIT, MOST LIBERATED FROM ANY OATH OF DUTY
OR OF CONSTANCY.

FRANCINE DU PLESSIX GRAY

A blessed thing it is for any man or woman to have a friend; one human soul
whom we can trust utterly; who knows the best and the worst of us,
and who loves us in spite of all our faults; who will speak the honest truth to us,
while the world flatters us to our face, and laughs at us behind our back;
who will give us counsel and reproof in the day of prosperity and self-conceit;
but who, again, will comfort and encourage us in the day of difficulty and
sorrow, when the world leaves us alone to fight our own battle as we can.

CHARLES KINGSLEY
(1819-1875)

In the world of relationships, possibly the most complicated, uncommon, hard to find, hard to keep, and most rewarding has got to be friendship. I speak as a woman whose life to a large degree has centered on and depended on friends – one whose feeling of belonging has come from the continuity of friendship. As I reflect on my life, I see that from the not so advanced age of twenty on, it is friends that have been the continuing thread – my connection with where I am, with where I have been, where I am going; my need, sometimes my cushion, sometimes my confidante. They have made me laugh, moved me to tears, hurt me, helped me, changed me. Extraordinary that I have been so lucky.

LAUREN BACALL, b.1924,
FROM "NOW"

Oh, the comfort, the inexpressible comfort,
of feeling safe with a person; having neither
to weigh thoughts nor measure words,
but to pour them all out just as they are,
chaff and grain together,
knowing that a faithful hand will take and sift them,
keep what is worth keeping,
and then, with the breath of kindness,
blow the rest away.

GEORGE ELIOT (MARY ANN EVANS)
(1819-1880)

Like the shade of a great tree in the noonday heat is a friend.
Like the home port with your country's flag flying
after a long journey is a friend. A friend is an impregnable citadel
of refuge in the strife of existence.

AUTHOR UNKNOWN

Long friendships are like jewels,
polished over time to become
beautiful and enduring.

CELIA BRAYFIELD

To the young, friendship comes
as the glory of the spring,
a very miracle of beauty, a mystery
of birth: to the old it has
the bloom of autumn,
beautiful still.

HUGH BLACK

Beautiful and rich
is an old friendship,
Grateful to the touch as
ancient ivory,
Smooth as aged wine, or
sheen of tapestry
Where light has lingered,
intimate and long.

EUNICE TIETJENS (1884-1944)
FROM "OLD FRIENDSHIPS"

One needs

different people in one's life...

simply to pay a visit

because it is such

a beautiful day.

K . D E P O O R T E R E

Even the utmost goodwill and harmony and practical

kindness are not sufficient for friendship, for friends do not live

in harmony merely, as some say, but in melody. We do not wish

for friends to feed and clothe our bodies – neighbors are kind

enough for that – but to do the like office to our spirits.

HENRY DAVID THOREAU
(1 8 1 7 - 1 8 6 2)

It is a mistake to think that one makes a friend
because of his or her qualities, it has nothing to do with qualities at all.
It is the person that we want, not what he does or says,
or does not do or say, but what he or she is that is eternally enough!
Who shall explain the extraordinary instinct that tells us,
perhaps after a single meeting, that this or that particular person
in some mysterious way matters to us?

ARTHUR CHRISTOPHER BENSON
(1 8 6 2 - 1 9 2 5)

We drop like pebbles
into the ponds
of each other's souls....

JOAN BORYSENKO

ONLY SOLITARY MEN

KNOW THE FULL JOYS OF FRIENDSHIP.

OTHERS HAVE THEIR FAMILY;

BUT TO A SOLITARY AND AN EXILE HIS FRIENDS

ARE EVERYTHING.

WILLA CATHER
(1876-1947)
FROM "SHADOWS ON THE ROCK"

A MAN WITHOUT FRIENDS IS LIKE A LEFT HAND

WITHOUT A RIGHT.

SOLOMON IBN GABIROL,
FROM "CHOICE OF PEARLS"

To others, we will be seen as two old biddies

kicking off their shoes, dumping down shopping bags,

choosing lethal pastries.

But to each other we are ourselves, a little scarred

by the passing years, but still the girls who shared

a bag of toffee on the playground wall,

we at least are not deceived by skin, spectacles

and silvery hair.

two old biddies

PAM BROWN, b.1928

There is a moment of solid conspiratorial silence, and then the three of them burst out laughing. Not one of them understands the reason for this sudden hilarity; it's just something that descends on them sometimes, like gusts of weather. ... Sometimes Daisy thinks that she and Fraidy and Beans are like one person sitting around in the same body, breathing in the same wafts of air and coming out with the same larky thoughts. This has been going on forever, all the years they were at Tudor Hall in Indianapolis, and then going off to Long College together, and pledging the same sorority and getting their diplomas on the same June morning. And whenever Daisy stops and thinks about her honeymoon, about actually standing in front of the Eiffel Tower or the Roman Coliseum, she always somehow imagines that Fraidy and Beans will be there too, standing right next to her and whooping and laughing and racketing around like crazy.

CAROL SHIELDS, FROM "THE STONE DIARIES"

*One of the most beautiful
qualities of true friendship is
to understand and to be understood.*

SENECA (c.55 B.C.-c.40 A.D.)

Miraculously, our most serious situations seem to lighten when
we tell them to a friend and feel that she has heard us. The
magic happens when a friend is able to put herself in our place
and, knowing us as she does, to help us come to a decision
without necessarily solving the problem for us. Being heard is a
clarifying potion – not made by any cosmetics company – that
helps us to see things clearly.

CARMEN RENEE BERRY AND TAMARA TRAEDER, FROM "GIRLFRIENDS"

The friends who listen to us
are the ones we move toward,
and we want to sit in their radius.
When we are listened to,
it creates us, makes us unfold
and expand.

KARL MENNINGER

It is said that love is blind.

Friendship, on the other

hand, is clairvoyant.

PHILIP SOUPAULT

MY FRIEND

My friend is
like bark
rounding a tree
he warms
like sun
on a winter day
he cools
like water
in the hot noon
his voice
is ready
as a spring bird
he is
my friend
and I
am his

*EMILY HEARN,
FROM "HOCKEY CARDS AND HOPSCOTCH"*

Our friendships are...
the structures that hold us in place
when our world threatens
to dissolve.

ROSALYN CHISSICK,
FROM "NEW WOMAN", AUGUST 1994

When the willow bends at the first hint of troubled breezes,

our friends come running to see how they can help.

Sometimes friends know when they are needed

even before we realize it ourselves,

because we are accustomed to letting them in on

the happenings of our lives.

LOIS WYSE

Old friends stay the same age forever.

PAM BROWN, b.1928

With an old friend you can be more authentic than with anyone else.
You probably know everything there is to know about each other,
there is no need for pretence, or explanation.
Instead, you have the shared experiences, crazy memories
and deep understanding.

CELIA BRAYFIELD,
FROM "WOMAN AND HOME", OCTOBER 1997

None of us are as young
as we were. So what?
Friendship never ages.

W.H. AUDEN
(1907-1973)

That is the kingliness of friendship. We meet like sovereign princes of independent states, abroad, on neutral ground, freed from our contexts. This love (essentially) ignores not only our physical bodies but that whole embodiment which consists of our family, job, past and connections. At home, besides being Peter or Jane, we also bear a general character; husband or wife, brother or sister, chief, colleague or subordinate. Not among our friends. It is an affair of disentangled, or stripped, minds. Eros will have naked bodies; friendship naked personalities.

C . S .   L E W I S   (1 8 9 8 - 1 9 6 3)

among friends

Friendship needs no words –
it is solitude delivered
from the anguish of loneliness.

DAG HAMMARSKJÖLD
(1905-1961)

He who, silent, loves to be with us, and who loves us
in our silence, has touched
one of the keys that warm hearts.

JOHN C. LAVATER

That friendship only is, indeed, genuine when two friends,
without speaking a word to each other, can, nevertheless,
find happiness in being together.

GEORG EBERS
(1837-1898)

There were probably twenty gestating women in the room but it looked like 120. All waddling between rows of chairs, cradling their huge lumps. It looked like an ostrich farm. Liz Woolman and I exchanged pleasantries and sat down to listen to the words of wisdom which issued from the expert on painless birth. After ten minutes of baby voice on the "ickle woman" and the "big daddy man" we caught each other's eyes, rolled them skywards and gave birth to a friendship based on instant bullshit detection.... From that day, we've been each other's salvation. Nobody wanted babies more than we did but equally we needed stimulating conversation and a good moan about loss of liberty and sleep. ... What we had in common was how unfinished we still were. Perhaps are.

Since then she's been my sounding board. ... I trust her with all my nastiest bits because I know she'll like me anyway. ... We are both opinionated and judgmental and know that we can be alarming to others, but I guess, together, we cancel out each other's bossiness. I am blessed with all my girlfriends but the best blessing was that bloody awful "breathing for birth" bash, where my chum and I first rolled our eyes towards the heavens and got bonded.

MAUREEN LIPMAN,
FROM "THE EXPRESS ON SUNDAY", OCTOBER 27, 1996

ABOUT FRIENDS

The good thing about friends is not having to finish sentences.

I sat a whole summer afternoon with my friend once on a river bank,
bashing heels on the baked mud and watching the small chunks slide
into the water and listening to them – plop plop plop.
He said "I like the twigs when they... you know... like that."
I said "There's that branch..."
We both said "Mmmm". The river flowed and flowed
and there were lots of butterflies, that afternoon.

I first thought there was a sad thing about friends
when we met twenty years later.
We both talked hundreds of sentences, taking care to
finish all we said, and explain it all very carefully,
as if we'd been discovered in places we should not be,
and were somehow ashamed.

I understood then what the river meant by flowing.

BRIAN JONES

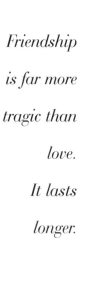

Friendship

is far more

tragic than

love.

It lasts

longer.

OSCAR WILDE
(1854-1900)

*N*ever exaggerate your faults;
your friends will attend to that.

CICERO (106-43 B.C.)

We are so fond of one another,
because our ailments are the same.

JONATHAN SWIFT (1667-1745)

But of all plagues, good Heaven, thy wrath can send,
Save me, oh, save me, from the candid friend.

GEORGE CANNING (1770-1827)

Anybody can sympathize
with the sufferings of a friend,
but it requires a very fine nature to sympathize
with a friend's success.

OSCAR WILDE (1854-1900)

For what is your friend that you should seek
him with hours to kill?
Seek him always with hours to live.
For it is his to fill your need,
not your emptiness.
And in the sweetness of friendship let there
be laughter and sharing of pleasures.

KAHLIL GIBRAN (1883-1931)

... no one ever told me what a wonderful thing friendship would be.
I remember when I was about seventeen years old,
lying in my best friend's garden feeling exquisitely happy
just to be with her. We were discovering the world together,
making up the rules for ourselves, creating our own little universe
of tastes, preferences and morals. And jokes.
Remember laughing out of control about absolutely nothing?
We did lots of that.
At the back of my mind, I assumed that we would grow
out of the joy of teenage friendship, and we did.
What I did not expect was that it would be replaced
by something altogether more magnificent,
which rivals and even surpasses most of life's other pleasures.
It is only now that I really understand how precious
friendship can be.

CELIA BRAYFIELD,
FROM "WOMAN AND HOME", OCTOBER 1997

Who else but a friend will listen for hours on end,

day after day, while you disinter every last bitter second

of a shattered relationship, and who else but a friend,

a good friend, will one day suggest, very gently,

that maybe it's time to turn the page and move on?

ANNE WOODHAM,
FROM "GOOD HOUSEKEEPING", NOVEMBER 1997

A REAL FRIEND
NEVER GETS IN YOUR WAY.
UNLESS YOU HAPPEN TO BE
ON THE WAY DOWN.

AUTHOR UNKNOWN

and to accept
kindness

One who knows how to show and to accept kindness
will be a friend better than any possession.

SOPHOCLES
(c.496-405 B.C.)

How often have we built each other as shelters

against the cold.

AUDRE LORDE

If after I go out a friend of mine gave a feast, and did not invite me to it, I shouldn't mind a bit. ... But if, after I go out, a friend of mine had a sorrow, and refused to allow me to share it, I should feel it most bitterly. If he shut the doors of the house of mourning against me I would come back again and again and beg to be admitted, so that I might share in what I was entitled to share in. If he thought me unworthy, unfit to weep with him, I should feel it... as the most terrible mode in which disgrace could be inflicted on me.

OSCAR WILDE (1854-1900)

THERE IS A DESTINY THAT MAKES US BROTHERS:
NONE GOES HIS WAY ALONE;
ALL THAT WE SEND INTO
THE LIVES OF OTHERS COMES
BACK INTO OUR OWN.

EDWIN MARKHAM

When we were very small we played together under the summer trees, picked dandelions to carry home, drew in the dust of shadowed lanes, stamped in mud, kicked joyfully through Autumn leaves.

Age was no concern of ours. The seasons gave their gifts and gave no hint that time would mark us.

But the trees are felled, the meadows vanished, the lanes forgotten.

And we are growing old, my friend. Walk with me, then, and talk of those lost times – still vivid in our minds. Still living in our hearts.

Life is still good – but we live in both worlds.

We recognize the children that we were shining in one another's eyes.

And smile – knowing that nothing good is ever lost.

PAM BROWN, b.1928

... friends... should be able, no, eager, to sit for hours – three, four, six – over a meal of soup and wine and cheese, as well as one of twenty fabulous courses. Then, with good friends of such attributes, and good food on the board, and good wine in the pitcher, we may well ask, when shall we live if not now?

M.F.K. FISHER, FROM "THE ART OF EATING"

... the conversation of friends... is the nearest approach we can make to heaven while we live in these tabernacles of clay; so it is in a temporal sense also, the most pleasant and the most profitable improvement we can make of the time we are to spend on earth.

RACHEL RUSSELL (1636-1723)

If a true friendship can be found,
cherish it like a fine gem. Polish it, go
out of your way to keep and protect it.
Keep it safe, but let it shine for itself.
It will grow and grow.

MARY SWANEY

chain of gold

MY FRIEND!

YOU YOURSELF ARE MY TREASURE,

THE CHAIN OF GOLD AROUND MY NECK.

BENGALI FOLK SONG

Being a friend, I do not care, not I,

How gods or men wrong me, beat me down.

His words are a sufficient star to travel by.

I count him with quiet praise.

Being a friend, I do not covet gold,

Or the royal gift to give him pleasure, but

sit with him and have him hold my hand.

Is wealth, I think, passing the mint treasure?

Being a friend, I only covet art,

A white pure flame to search me as I trace,

In crooked letters from a throbbing heart,

The hymn to beauty written on his face.

A I D S   P A T I E N T

IF I SHOULD MEET THEE
AFTER LONG YEARS,
HOW SHOULD I GREET THEE?
WITH SILENCE AND TEARS.

LORD BYRON
(1788-1824)

Ships that pass in the night,
and speak each other in passing,
Only a signal shown,
and a distant voice in the darkness;
So on the ocean of life,
we pass and speak one another,
Only a look and a voice,
then darkness again and a silence.

HENRY WADSWORTH LONGFELLOW
(1807-1882)

The world is so wide and each of us so small –
yet bound by friendship we are giants.

PAM BROWN, b.1928

When [friends] are real,
they are not glass threads
or frost-work,
but the solidest thing we know.

RALPH WALDO EMERSON (1803-1882)

... absence will not seem an evil
If it makes our re-meeting
A real occasion. Come when you can:
Your room will be ready.

W.H. AUDEN (1907-1973)

... I never weary of watching for you on the road.
... Oh that I could shrink the surface of the world,
So that suddenly I might find you standing at my side!

WANG-CHIEN

There are red-letter days in our lives when we meet people
who thrill us like a fine poem, people whose handshake is brimful
of unspoken sympathy and whose sweet, rich natures impart to our
eager, impatient spirits a wonderful restfulness... the influence
of their calm, mellow natures is a libation poured
upon our discontent....

HELEN KELLER
(1880-1968)

SOME PEOPLE COME INTO OUR LIVES
AND QUICKLY GO...
SOME PEOPLE STAY FOR A WHILE
AND LEAVE THEIR FOOTPRINTS
ON OUR HEARTS,
AND WE ARE NEVER, EVER THE SAME.

FLAVIA

Happiness is the whole world as friends.
It's light all through your life.

DANIEL DILLING, AGE 8

At every stage of my life friendship has
been the main source of my quite
outrageously enjoyable existence.

SIR GEOFFREY KEYNES

*Laughter is not at all
a bad beginning for a friendship,
and it is by far the best ending
for one.*

OSCAR WILDE
(1854-1900)

I WANT TO BE YOUR FRIEND

FOR EVER AND EVER WITHOUT BREAK OR DECAY.

WHEN THE HILLS ARE ALL FLAT

AND THE RIVERS ARE ALL DRY,

WHEN IT LIGHTENS AND THUNDERS IN WINTER,

WHEN IT RAINS AND SNOWS IN SUMMER,

WHEN HEAVEN AND EARTH MINGLE —

NOT TILL THEN WILL I PART FROM YOU.

CHINESE OATH OF FRIENDSHIP,
FIRST CENTURY A.D.

PICTURE CREDITS

TEXT CREDITS

Acknowledgements: The publishers are grateful for permission to reproduce copyright material. Whilst every reasonable effort has been made to trace copyright holders, the publishers would be pleased to hear from any not here acknowledged.

W.H. AUDEN: "Shorts" from *Collected Poems* published by Faber and Faber Ltd, 1994 © 1974 by the Estate of W. H. Auden. Reprinted by permission of Random House Inc. Extract from "For Friends Only" from *About the House*, published by Faber and Faber Ltd, 1966 © 1940 and renewed 1968 by W. H. Auden: Reprinted by permission of Random House Inc.

LAUREN BACALL: From *Now* by Lauren Bacall, published by Hutchinson, © 1994. Reprinted by permission of Random House Ltd.

PAM BROWN, © Helen Exley, 1998.

CARMEN RENEE BERRY AND TAMARA TRAEDER: From *Girlfriends: Invisible Bonds, Enduring Ties* © 1995 Carmen Renee Berry and Tamara C. Traeder. Reprinted with permission of Wildcat Press, a division of Circulus Publishing Group, Inc. All rights reserved.

KAHLIL GIBRAN: From *The Prophet*, © 1923 Kahlil Gibran, renewed 1951 by Administrators C.T.A. of Kahlil Gibran Estate and Mary C. Gibran. With permission from Alfred A. Knopf Inc.

EMILY HEARN: "My Friend" from *Hockey Cards and Hopscotch*, by John McInnes and Emily Hearn. Published by Nelson Canada. Used with permission of the author.

BRIAN JONES: "About Friends" from *A Spitfire on the Northern Line*, published by The Bodley Head. Used with permission.

ELIZABETH JENNINGS: From "Friendship" from *New Poems 1970-71*, ed. Alan Brownjohn, Seamus Heaney, and Jon Stallworthy. Published by Hutchinson. Reprinted with permission of David Higham Associates.

HELEN KELLER: "Red Letter Days" from *My Religion*, published by The Swedenbourg Foundation, 1960.

C.S. LEWIS: From *The Four Loves* by C.S. Lewis. © 1960 Helen Joy Lewis and renewed 1988 by Arthur Owen Barfield. Reprinted with permission of HarperCollins Publishers Ltd and Harcourt Brace and Company.

MAUREEN LIPMAN: From the article, *Born Friends*, in "The Express on Sunday" October 1996. Used with permission of the author.

HENRY ALONZO MYERS: From *Are Men Equal? An Inquiry into the Meaning of American Democracy*. © 1945 H.A. Myers, published by Cornell University Press.

CAROL SHIELDS: From *The Stone Diaries* published by Fourth Estate. © Carol Shields 1993. Used with permission of Fourth Estate Ltd, Viking Penguin, a division of Penguin Putnam, Inc and Random House of Canada Ltd.